THE ALNWICK GARDEN

CONTENTS

FOREWORD

I THINK OF THE ALNWICK GARDEN in human terms. Even in dereliction I could sense its soul, and archaeological surveys undertaken as we made the new garden identified the remains of six earlier gardens underneath. The garden has evolved with time, as both people and gardens do. I remember it so well in its neglected state - it was tragic, but the bones of something majestic were there, and I knew it could be resuscitated and made relevant to the twenty-first century.

The Alnwick Garden is so much more than just another garden to visit. It is a place of happiness and laughter, built to be loved and used by the local community. Children splash in the water displays and ride the toy tractors parked below the Grand Cascade; through watching and interacting with the various water features, they learn that science can be fun. In the Poison Garden, trained storytellers entertain and educate, showing how plants have killed throughout history, and passing on valuable drug awareness messages. Elderly visitors take advantage of the tea dances, exercise classes and other services we offer them; school parties learn to grow fruit and vegetables in the Roots and Shoots garden; and all ages love the Treehouse. Sometimes I watch a group of elderly people laughing their way along 20-metre-high wobbly rope bridges and I realise that age is no barrier to pleasure.

The Alnwick Garden has become a contemporary pleasure garden, bringing joy in so many ways to so many people from all walks of life. To me a garden without people is dead, and people have brought the Alnwick Garden to life and restored its soul.

THE DUCHESS OF NORTHUMBERLAND

INTRODUCTION

THE ALNWICK GARDEN is one of the most exciting contemporary gardens to be developed anywhere in the world in the last 100 years. Inspired by the Duchess of Northumberland and designed by the world-renowned Belgian landscape firm of Wirtz International, the garden's centrepiece is the Grand Cascade, a magnificent tumbling mass of water surrounded by cool hornbeam arbours.

Beyond the Cascade is the geometric Ornamental Garden, with inviting pathways bordered by lavender and fruit trees, and hidden benches to catch the sun. On either side are individually conceived garden spaces and structures – the fragrant Rose Garden, the mysterious Bamboo Labyrinth, the sinuous Serpent Garden and the grim, locked Poison Garden – linked by a network of green shapes and brought to life by water features. The flowing landscape that results is a fascinating sequence of quiet and busy spaces, and full of surprises.

The Alnwick Garden is also home to one of the world's largest wooden treehouses, high in the trees and featuring rope bridges and walkways in the sky. The Treehouse restaurant offers lunch and dinner, while the sheltered terrace of the Pavilion is a lovely place to sit and watch the Grand Cascade, over coffee, lunch or afternoon tea.

In the ten years since it first opened to the public, the Alnwick Garden has attracted huge publicity and media interest, and become a key player in the local and regional economy, attracting 320,000 visits in its first year and over 800,000 in 2011. It won the Northumbrian Tourist Board's Large Visitor Attraction of the Year award in 2003, and the EU Partners in Europe Pride of the Region award in 2006.

Designed to appeal at every season and to evolve with the changing year, the garden is still being developed, with five further gardens planned. This, together with a diverse programme of events for all ages, ensures that there is always something new to see and something interesting to do in the Alnwick Garden.

Below: The Grand Cascade is dramatically illuminated at night.

HISTORY OF THE GARDEN

THE FIRST GARDEN ON THIS SITE, located close to Alnwick Castle, the ancestral home of the Percy family, was begun in 1750 by Hugh Percy, who became the first Duke of Northumberland in 1766. The boundary walls, enclosing a 12-acre enclosure that is the present garden, were built from 1777 using bricks transported to Alnwick as ship-ballast.

The third Duke was a keen plant collector and he transformed Alnwick into a garden of flowers, building a large conservatory on the site of the present Pavilion. In the mid-nineteenth century the fourth Duke created an Italianate garden here, reflecting the Italian Renaissance works he acquired for the State Rooms in Alnwick Castle. The earth banks on each side of the Grand Cascade were constructed at this time. The garden was considered to be at its grandest at the end of the nineteenth century, with topiary features and abundant floral displays.

In 1942, during World War II, the garden became an allotment and it remained in limited use as a kitchen garden until 1950, when the present Duke's father transferred it to the Estate Forestry Department. It was then used as a tree nursery until 1996, when the Duchess of Northumberland made the decision to restore the site and make 'a garden with a difference'.

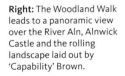

Right: The Woodland Walk leads to a panoramic view over the River Aln, Alnwick Castle and the rolling landscape laid out by 'Capability' Brown.

A GARDEN TO EXPLORE

GRAND CASCADE

THE CURVILINEAR GRAND CASCADE forms the centrepiece of Belgian designer Jacques Wirtz's garden design for Alnwick. It was one of the first features to be created, along with the Ornamental Garden, the Rose Garden and the Woodland Walk, in the first phase of development, which was formally opened in 2001.

One of the largest water features of its kind, the three-tiered Cascade occupies the main north-south axis and forms the spine of the garden. It is surrounded by topiary hornbeam hedges, which give height and substance and provide a rich green backdrop to the hard landscaping of the Cascade. The water feature itself is almost wholly constructed in the local Northumbrian sandstone, except for the internal wall facings, which are made of coloured and moulded concrete to protect against wear from the water. The half-hourly water display uses 120 water jets, 40 on each side and 40 down the centre. Four further powerful jets propel spouts of water over the main terrace that straddles the Cascade and into the Lower Basin, the pool at the base of the Cascade, which in turn activates a water display simulating a volcanic eruption.

Pumps, filters and treatment systems are all housed in two vast plant rooms beneath the Cascade, together with reservoirs which also supply the water for the pools, ponds and water sculptures in adjoining features, with all water recycled and re-used. The engineering work associated with the Cascade won the Institution of Civil Engineers Robert Stephenson Award in 2002.

ENGINEERING FACTS:

- 21 weirs keep the water flowing
- 120 water jets create the display
- 250,000 gallons of water circulate through the system
- 850 hornbeam trees are planted around the perimeter
- innovative lighting and audio effects at night

Left: Four different water sequences are programmed into the Cascade computer system.

Right: This aerial view emphasises the sinuous curves of the Cascade and the rippling hornbeam hedging that surrounds it. Part of the Serpent Garden can be seen at bottom right.

Above: The design of the Cascade takes advantage of the natural slope of the landscape.

Left: Looking through the hornbeam hedging to jets of water playing in the air.

Right: All the water flowing through the complex Cascade system is recycled; here it takes on the mellow glow of the Northumbrian stone.

Below: The view from above the Cascade at night, looking down towards the welcoming warmth of the Pavilion.

ORNAMENTAL GARDEN

THIS WALLED SPACE was the original kitchen garden for the Castle, but became a larch seed orchard when the garden was taken over by the Estate Forestry Department. It is now designed as a series of 'rooms', each one framed by carefully selected shrubs and espaliered trees. In one area, *Cornus mas* (dogwood) hedging encloses several European varieties of cream-coloured hydrangeas, which are allowed to grow above the hedge-level to create a shaped 'ceiling' over the 'room'. The central spaces are enclosed by espaliered *Malus* 'Red Sentinel' (crab apple), while the low-growing *Malus* 'Evereste' forms clipped hedges as a backdrop to triangular borders. The first tree to be introduced here in the north border as part of the new design was planted by the Duchess in memory of the present Duke's nanny.

At the centre of the Ornamental Garden lies a bubbling pool, the Source Pool, spilling into shallow rills that are perfect for splashing and paddling. The rills feed two mirrored pools which are enclosed in yew hedges to form further 'rooms'. The water movement is created by flap valves releasing air which in turn forms bubbles that rise to the surface

KEY FACTS
- Over 16,000 plants
- The Venetian gates date from the sixteenth century

Left: The pergola surrounding the Source Pool supports climbing roses, clematis and honeysuckle, providing a scented canopy above the welcoming seats.

Right: The fine wrought-iron sixteenth-century gates were bought by the fourth Duke in Italy during the 1850s and restored by local Northumbrian specialists in 2000.

ROSE GARDEN

The Rose Garden, sponsored by David Austin Roses, features over 3000 English shrub roses and climbers, and 200 different species. Most notably, these include the exquisite Alnwick Rose, launched at the Chelsea Flower Show in 2001.

Pergola-lined pathways lead through the garden, offering a heady vista of glorious and fragrant blooms from May right through to early winter. The pergola used here is a feature of Jacques Wirtz's design for the Rose Garden and supports clematis and honeysuckle as well as climbing and rambling roses. The rose bushes are pruned on a three-year cycle, to create a flowing and harmonious visual experience throughout the blooming period.

Left: The *Fox* sculpture at the centre of the Rose Garden was made originally for Painshill Park in Surrey, c.1750, and was bought by the present Duke's father.

Below left: The varying height of the rose bushes in the borders is an integral part of the garden design; the varieties chosen provide a harmony of colour and a symphony of fragrance.

Right: Four of the David Austin roses that feature in the Rose Garden (clockwise from top left): Grace, a Leander hybrid; Falstaff, an Old Rose hybrid; The Alnwick Rose, noted for its wonderful fruity fragrance; Ferdinand Pichard, a repeat-flowering Old Rose.

WOODLAND WALK

IN CONTRAST to the more formal areas of the garden, the Woodland Walk offers a naturally undulating pathway, shaded by mature trees and leading down to the River Aln. In spring the path is enriched with wildflowers and heavy with the scent of wild garlic, and in summer the sun shining though the canopy of leaves creates a cool, dappled effect. The rich colours of autumn are a feast for the eye, while in winter the bare skeletons of the trees make dramatic shapes.

The walk can be accessed from the disabled car park and gives outstanding views of Alnwick Castle and the surrounding landscape, designed by the great eighteenth-century landscape architect 'Capability' Brown. Within the woodland are activity areas used by local schools and clubs to give the younger generation the opportunity to experience and understand the importance of conserving and protecting the rural environment.

Left and far right: The Woodland Walk, leading down to the River Aln, provides a visual link with the wooded parklands created by 'Capability' Brown in the eighteenth century for the first Duke of Northumberland.

Below: The woodland area is devoted to wildlife conservation and features some very sophisticated nesting boxes.

Right: Here tree-trunks create an almost abstract pattern.

SERPENT GARDEN

Below: The *Meniscus* water sculpture illustrates the convex upper surface formed by liquid in a container, caused by surface tension.

Below: The *Meniscus* water sculpture illustrates the convex upper surface formed by liquid in a container, caused by surface tension.

THE SERPENT GARDEN forms part of the second phase of development at Alnwick, opened in 2005. A serpent shape formed of *Lonicera nitida* 'Baggesen's Gold' meanders its way through this garden, its tail starting near the Pavilion and its coils embracing a sequence of seven water sculptures designed by William Pye. Each of these sculptures explores a different aspect of the behaviour of water, forming a subtle physics lesson. Here children can simultaneously learn and get wet!

At the serpent's head is a circular paved area in which the water sculpture *Torricelli* rises into the sky, illustrating water under hydrostatic pressure – the water rises in the transparent tubes until it is level with the surface of the square source pool in the Mulberry Garden above, and 90 jets leap and subside in unison with the water level.

The Mulberry Garden, like the sculptures, is enclosed by a clipped yew hedge. The stepped detail below the hedge is in beech, a formal shape but one which echoes the flowing beech hedging on each side, creating a natural link between formal and free-flowing areas of the garden.

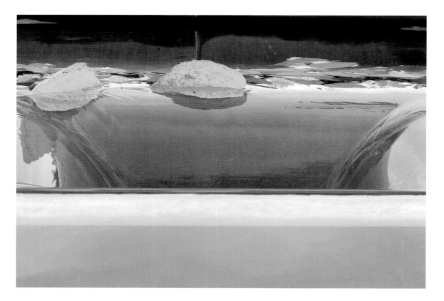

Left: The pool in the Mulberry Garden feeds the *Torricelli* water sculpture in the Serpent Garden.

Right: The *Torricelli* sculpture shows water under hydrostatic pressure – and its 90 leaping jets of water are irresistible to children.

BAMBOO LABYRINTH

Designed by maze-maker Adrian Fisher and set in a windy area of the garden, the Bamboo Labyrinth sways and rustles above the brick paths that wander between its green walls, confusing and perplexing the visitor. The Labyrinth is planted with *Fargesia rufa*, a new type of bamboo introduced from China, which is hardy against drought and keeps its delicate green leaves in winter. The plants are set into raised banks, formed of compressed peat blocks from a sustainable source in Poland. The surface of the paths is ornamented with delicate bronze details, representing bamboo leaves floating in the stream.

The boulder placed at the entrance was brought from a hillside in Hulne Park, part of the Alnwick estate, to provide a welcome to the Labyrinth. It is inscribed with the phrase 'Only dead fish swim with the stream', a neat summary of the garden's aim of avoiding the conventional route and searching out new challenges and innovative approaches.

Left: The curving paths of the Bamboo Labyrinth merge and divide like a stream.

Above: The Latin inscription on the paving at the exit point can be translated as 'Visitors, you have seen it all, we thank you, now go happily on your way'.

Left: Alnwick's challenging maxim, at the entrance to the Labyrinth.

THE POISON GARDEN

THESE PLANTS CAN KILL

POISON GARDEN

ANOTHER PARTICULARLY POPULAR innovation introduced as part of the Phase 2 development, the Poison Garden is packed with dangerous plants, from belladonna and hemlock to tobacco and mandrake, and has a licence from the Home Office to grow cannabis and coca. Entry to the Poison Garden is through giant locked gates featuring the skull and crossbones; visitors are forbidden to smell, taste or touch, and must be accompanied by a guide, who will identify the various lethal plants and describe their sinister uses.

A combination of dark, ivy-covered tunnels and flame-shaped beds creates an educational garden full of interest and intrigue, where the most dangerous plants are kept within giant cages. But plants like these become killers only in the hands of men, and the Poison Garden is also a place where people of all ages can learn more about dangerous drugs and the pernicious effects they have on people's lives.

The Garden also features many plants grown unwittingly in back gardens, and which can be found in the British countryside. How much do you know about the plants you grow? The Poison Garden gives a fascinating glimpse into the darker side of nature.

Above: The flame-shaped beds inside the Poison Garden provide a suitably dramatic setting for their sinister contents.

Below left and right: Two poisonous plants, *Digitalis purpurea* (foxglove) and *Heracleum mantegazzianum* (giant hogweed).

Left (clockwise from top left): The imposing gates to the Poison Garden bear a stark warning; the Hovel, which stands by the Poison Garden, is a spooky little apothecary's hut; poisonous laburnum hangs over one of the giant cages in which the most dangerous plants are grown.

PAVILION AND VISITOR CENTRE

THE STUNNING MODERN BUILDINGS through which the visitor enters the garden were designed by acclaimed British architect Sir Michael Hopkins and opened to the public in 2006. The Visitor Centre is built around the original main courtyard just outside the garden, and includes gift shop, admissions and information, refreshments and meeting rooms.

The Pavilion inside the garden walls is designed to serve as the auditorium from which the drama of the garden can begin to be experienced, offering an immediate and stunning view of the Grand Cascade. The Pavilion's barrel-vaulted timber roof is covered with lightweight 'pillows', their shape echoing both the curvilinear flow of the Cascade and the undulating topiary planting throughout the garden. Terraces extend on either side, linking the Pavilion with the landscape of the garden, and a10-metre tall fastigiate beech 'tower' on the west terrace creates a focal point in the topiary structure of the Lower Garden.

The Pavilion building was the regional winner of the Royal Institute of British Architects award for architecture in 2008.

KEY FACTS

- Fibre-optic lighting set in the floor of the terraces and atrium creates a twinkling effect at dusk

- Heating and air conditioning supplied by an environmentally-friendly system based on a 90-metre borehole

- Toilets use recycled 'grey' water

Left: At night the lightweight air-filled membranes that form the Pavilion roof take on a glowing diaphanous appearance.

Above right: The structural frame of the Pavilion and its barrel-vaulted roof.

Right: The elegant Pavilion toilets won the 2006 UK Loo of the Year Award.

Far right: Fibre-optic lighting in the paving creates a twinkling effect at dusk.

TREEHOUSE

JUST OUTSIDE the garden's perimeter wall is perhaps the most surprising and exciting of all the surprises and excitements offered by the Alnwick Garden - one of the largest wooden treehouses in the world, winner of the Newcastle Journal Landmark Retail and Leisure Award 2005 and the Local Authority Building Control 2007 Award for innovatory disability access. It is built around 16 mature lime trees, which grow through and into the building but do not support the main structure; this is carried on piled foundations supported by raking timber columns. The timber used is a combination of Siberian larch, Scandinavian redwood, Canadian cedar, and Scots and English pine, all from sustainable sources.

The main level contains the 5*-rated Treehouse Restaurant, a catering service area, coffee bar and private function room, and there is an educational resource room in a self-contained treehouse adjoining the main promenade. The first stage of an amazing Play Area has been constructed off the main promenade, with walkways and rope suspension bridges linking towers among the trees. The Treehouse and Play Area are designed to meet access and activity requirements for all, including wheelchair users of all ages.

Left: In the next phase of work, these walkways will provide access to further activity features on different levels above the ground.

Above: The warm and welcoming interior of the Treehouse.

Right: The quirky design of the Treehouse masks its great size and makes it look well-established among the trees.

CHERRY ORCHARD

Left: Pink tulips and cherry blossom glow in the spring sunshine.

THE CHERRY ORCHARD, planted in 2008, is possibly the largest orchard in the world to feature the 'Tai-haku' tree, also known as the 'Great White'. A large and sturdy tree, it has huge snowlike clusters of blooms up to 7cm long, appearing in April at the same time as the coppery foliage, while in autumn it puts on a wonderful show of red and gold. All the 326 trees in the Cherry Orchard are available for visitors to sponsor.

The entire Orchard is under-planted with pink tulips 'The Mistress', creating a magical environment during the spring. Borders of *Rhododendron luteum* (azaleas), in white, yellow and orange, provide a continuous, highly-scented and colourful display through into summer, forming a boundary to the Cherry Orchard.

The serpentine path that loops and wanders its way slowly downhill through the Cherry Orchard is designed to meets the requirements of all, including wheelchair users, and provides an easy and meandering walk through this wonderful section of the garden.

The 'Tai-haku' was originally introduced to England in 1900, and was recognised years later in a Sussex garden by plant collector Captain Collingwood Ingram, after it had died out in Japan. Ingram became known as 'Cherry' Ingram, and was instrumental in re-introducing the tree to Japan. All the 'Tai-Haku' trees in the world are descended from the cuttings made by Cherry Ingram.

A GARDEN FOR ALL SEASONS

SPRING

Even before the official arrival of spring, there are bulbs in bloom at the Alnwick Garden. Bulb-planting has gathered pace here over the past decade; once they were counted in hundreds of thousands, but now it has become millions. The woodland leading to the Ornamental Garden is awash from late January with *Chionodoxa* (glory-of-the-snow), blue with white centre, the violet blue *Scilla siberica*, and many more.

The Cherry Orchard, with its under-planting of pink tulips, comes into its own in spring. The Ornamental Garden offers a stunning display of crab-apple blossom at eye-level and above, while at ground-level a range of herbaceous perennials welcomes the new season with colour. Two *Pulmonaria* (lungwort), 'Munstead Blue' and 'Sissinghurst White', look stunning against the dark earth background, as does *Erythronium* (dog-toothed violet).

Right: Crab-apple blossom lights up the Ornamental Garden in the delicate spring sunshine.

Below left: Snowdrops are the earliest sign of spring in the garden.

Below right: Camellias glow on the south-facing wall of the Ornamental Garden.

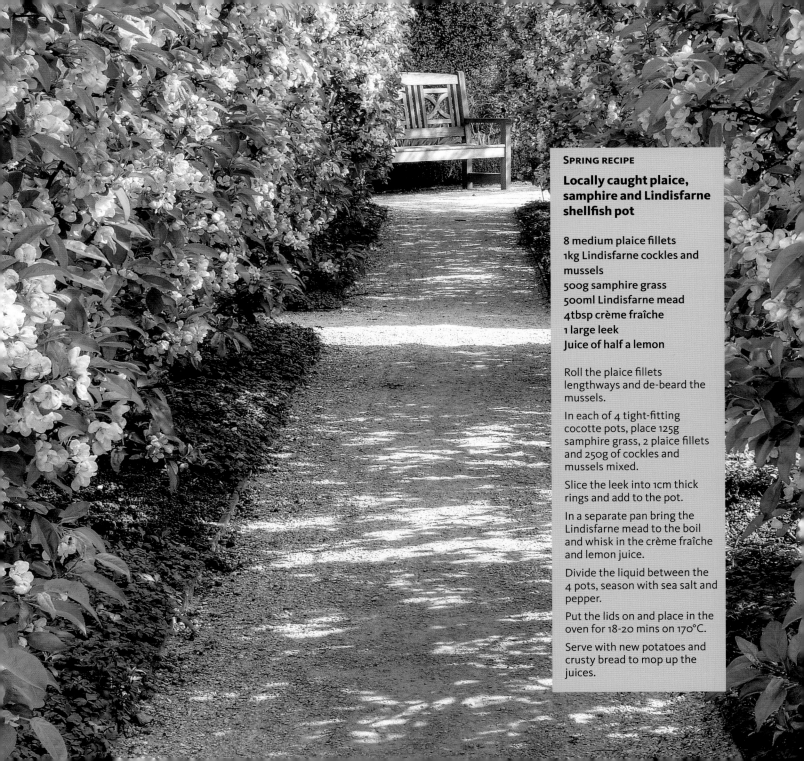

Locally caught plaice, samphire and Lindisfarne shellfish pot

8 medium plaice fillets
1kg Lindisfarne cockles and mussels
500g samphire grass
500ml Lindisfarne mead
4tbsp crème fraîche
1 large leek
Juice of half a lemon

Roll the plaice fillets lengthways and de-beard the mussels.

In each of 4 tight-fitting cocotte pots, place 125g samphire grass, 2 plaice fillets and 250g of cockles and mussels mixed.

Slice the leek into 1cm thick rings and add to the pot.

In a separate pan bring the Lindisfarne mead to the boil and whisk in the crème fraîche and lemon juice.

Divide the liquid between the 4 pots, season with sea salt and pepper.

Put the lids on and place in the oven for 18-20 mins on 170°C.

Serve with new potatoes and crusty bread to mop up the juices.

SUMMER

SUMMER BRINGS shrieks of childish delight to all corners of the lower Alnwick Garden as youngsters revel in getting wet, wet, wet! Adults perhaps prefer to sniff out the best fragrances in the Rose Garden, which offers its first and best display around the third week in June. And all generations seem to head for the Poison Garden, by now showcasing all its plant nastiness in glorious full growth.

Clematis, honeysuckle and roses adorn walls and pergolas in several parts of the garden, and represent the nicest possible assault on the senses. In summertime everything is larger than life, including the hydrangea cultivars to be found in the Ornamental Garden, which spill frothily out over the low hedge of *Cornus mas* (dogwood) that surrounds them.

Herbaceous perennials here attract a throng of butterflies and bees, summer-flowering clematis covers the eighteenth-century brick wall like a vast carpet, and there is surely nothing to touch the towering trumpet flowers of *Cardiocrinum giganteum* (giant Himalayan lily).

Right: Clematis scrambles up the brick walls of the Rose Garden while roses and perennials bloom in the borders below.

Below left: Clematis and climbing rose adorn the pergola in the Ornamental Garden.

Below right: *Papaver orientale* (oriental poppy).

Salad of rabbit and wood pigeon with pickled baby carrots and fresh peas

1 rabbit, jointed
4 pigeon breasts
16 baby carrots, peeled
200g fresh peas, shelled
1 head frisée lettuce
200g watercress
100ml cider vinegar
300ml rape seed oil
1tbsp Dijon mustard
1tbsp caster sugar
1 litre vegetable stock
Pickling liquor:
250ml water
250ml white wine vinegar
50g sugar
12 black peppercorns

Cover the rabbit with vegetable stock and heat to a simmer. Cook until falling off the bone (about 1½ hours).

Mix all pickling liquor ingredients together. Place in a pan with carrots. Bring to the boil, remove from heat and allow the carrots to cool in the liquor.

Blanch the fresh peas in boiling salted water for 2 minutes and refresh in iced water.

Make the dressing by thoroughly mixing the cider vinegar, rape seed oil, caster sugar and mustard.

Drain the rabbit and flake the meat. Cook the pigeon breasts in a frying pan until pink (2 minutes each side) and leave to rest.

To assemble the salad, drain the carrots and peas and place in a mixing bowl with the leaves, rabbit and sliced pigeon, coat with dressing, season, toss together, and divide between 4 plates.

Roasted butternut squash soup with sage oil

2 large butternut squash, peeled and diced
4 garlic cloves, crushed
2 thyme sprigs
1 large onion, diced
1 large potato, peeled and chopped
2 medium carrots
1 litre vegetable stock
200ml double cream
100ml extra virgin olive oil
4 sage sprigs

Put the olive oil in a saucepan with the sage and leave to infuse somewhere warm for as long as possible (overnight would be best).

Place the squash, garlic and thyme in a roasting tin, season with salt and pepper and a drizzle of olive oil, and place in a hot oven for 25 minutes

In a thick-bottomed pan, sweat the onion for 2 minutes, then add the carrots and the potato.

When the squash comes out of the oven, add to the pan with the other ingredients and enough vegetable stock just to cover.

Simmer for 30 minutes, blend, add the cream, season with salt and white pepper.

The soup should be quite thick and very smooth. Serve in a warm bowl and drizzle with sage oil.

AUTUMN

Left: The rich colours of autumn foliage in the Ornamental Garden.

Below: Glowing autumn hues in the Ornamental Garden.

Below right: The apple trees in the Roots and Shoots Garden provide a fine harvest.

A UTUMN MEANS FRUITS and colourful foliage in any garden and Alnwick is no exception. In the Roots and Shoots Garden, a hive of activity throughout the summer months, the vegetables can now be harvested. Embryo fruits on several roses in the Rose Garden, left during the summer dead-heading process which keeps new flowers coming, have now turned into large red hips. This is the time to go fruit-spotting in the Ornamental Garden and marvel at row upon row of crab apples as well as isolated individuals grown as specimen trees. Showiest of all is *Malus* 'Butterball', whose large clusters of cheerful yellow apples reflect the slightest hint of sunlight.

Then we have the prospect of colourful foliage at every turn, as deciduous trees and shrubs reabsorb valuable food elements from their leaves before they fall. This process creates an annual spectacle, prolonged by cold nights followed by warm days. The lime trees around which the Treehouse is built are generally the first to catch the eye. The purple leaves of the grapevine *Vitis vinifera* 'Purpurea' are short-lived and spectacular, but the beeches and hornbeams, so prominent from the Pavilion, are in for the long haul when it comes to autumn displays.

WINTER

WINTER LAYS MOST GARDENS BARE, but here at Alnwick leaf-fall reveals the underlying structures that form the elegant bones of this wonderful site. The steel pergola, masked in summer by rose, honeysuckle and clematis, still has them clinging in bare-leaf state as it meanders through the Rose Garden. The hornbeam tunnels that skirt the Grand Cascade retain their architectural definition, and even a few clinging leaves, in winter.

Further structural depth greets visitors to the Ornamental Garden, where tall, pleached standards of *Malus* 'Red Sentinel' (ornamental crab apple) carry the eye skywards, with yew enclosures and the criss-crossed rows of another crab, 'Evereste', lower down, and below them the lowly *Ilex crenata* (box-holly) hedges which surround the parterres. Fragrant winter shrubs, such as *Chimonanthus praecox* (wintersweet) and *Viburnum bodnantense* 'Dawn', perfume the air, while the most notable floral attraction at ground level is a series of ten hellebore varieties, all great survivors despite their elegant, even vulnerable, appearance. *Helleborus orientalis* 'Early Purple' is the first to bloom, in December, and before it fades in February the white *H. niger* (Christmas rose) and lime-green *H. Argutifolius* (Corsican hellebore) will have appeared.

Right: Pleached crab apple gives structure to the Ornamental Garden.

Below left: The first hellebore to bloom in winter is the richly coloured *Helleborus orientalis* 'Early Purple'.

Below: A winter covering of snow helps to emphasise the elegant flowing lines of the garden design.

Slow-cooked Northumbrian shin of beef in Alnwick IPA

1kg beef shin
250g shallots peeled and left whole
4 cloves garlic chopped
½ celeriac cut into 1cm cubes
2 tbsp Worcestershire sauce
1 500ml bottle Alnwick IPA
2 tbsp brown sugar
3 tbsp plain flour
2 medium carrots roughly chopped
3 thyme sprigs
1 tbsp tomato purée
1 litre beef stock
Salt and pepper
200g smoked bacon lardons

Coat the beef in the flour. Heat 2 tbsp vegetable oil in a thick-bottomed pan and quick-fry the beef in the pan until nicely browned, then remove from the pan and set aside.

In the same pan add the bacon lardons, shallots, carrots, celeriac and thyme and sweat for 3 minutes.

Stir in the tomato purée, sugar and a good pinch of salt and pepper, and cook for a further 2 minutes.

Place the beef back in the pan, add the beer and enough beef stock to just cover the ingredients and add the Worcestershire sauce.

Bring to a simmer, cover tightly, then place in the oven for 2½ hours at 160°C.

Serve with creamy mashed potato.

A GARDEN FOR EVERYONE

'This is a place of happiness and laughter. Older people sit on benches, smiling, watching children playing and running in and out of the water.' –
THE DUCHESS OF NORTHUMBERLAND

THE ALNWICK GARDEN TRUST

Left: The Hatter is just one of many entertainers who add to the joy of the garden.

Below: Making, growing and exploring is all part of the garden's appeal for young and old alike.

THE ALNWICK GARDEN offers even more to its visitors than a great day out. Operated as a charity by the Alnwick Garden Trust, it has a full programme of arts, education and family events. Over 55,000 visitors took part in educational activities and workshops in summer 2011 alone, and more than half a million have toured the Poison Garden in the last three years, increasing drug awareness.

The Trust places great emphasis on the importance of play for a healthy childhood, and the whole garden is focused on offering children the space and the opportunity for creative play. A specially-designed activities programme for families with disabled children offers the support and encouragement needed to make their visit easy and welcoming. The 'Elderberries' programme aims to address the common problem of loneliness in old age by providing opportunities for old people to get together to talk, sing, dance and just enjoy the glories of the garden.

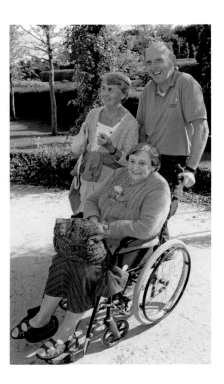

ROOTS AND SHOOTS GARDEN

ONE OF THE MOST SUCCESSFUL community programmes is the Roots and Shoots project, a productive fruit, vegetable and flower garden which is used as a teaching resource to inspire and delight all visitors, and above all children from deprived and inner-city areas, who have never known the joy of growing, picking and tasting fresh herbs, fruit and vegetables. The main aim of the project is to make learning about growing food fun, while raising awareness of the link between diet and health. From humble beginnings, where children learned to pot, plant and sow, and with generous sponsorship and donations from benefactors, the Roots and Shoots garden now houses two growing tunnels, raised beds, beehives, wormeries, a tipi, scarecrows, a fruit tunnel and many other quirky ways to grow plants. Ten schools have taken part in a year-long Roots and Shoots Academy programme to help them develop and maintain their own school garden, and more than 4000 children have enjoyed the 'Bee Friendly' programme during summer 2011, learning about the ecological importance of the honeybee.

Right: Salad plants create an appealing still-life in the Roots and Shoots garden.

Below: The joy of the harvest, whether it's tomatoes, onions or grapes.

GET INVOLVED

'To help someone fulfil a dream is truly a privilege' –
SUE SIMPSON, CHAIR OF VOLUNTEERS

THE ALNWICK GARDEN has attracted huge interest and support since its first opening in 2001. Donors choose to support the garden because they can identify with its values, as expressed through the work of the Alnwick Garden Trust. Sponsoring a tree in the Cherry Orchard in memory of a loved one has proved a popular and inspiring way of creating an eternal tribute in a garden that is so full of life and colour.

Becoming a Friend of the Garden helps to support the Garden's charitable projects and programmes through the Friends' subscription. Friends also enjoy access to the Garden all year round, free parking, and invitations to Friends events.

Volunteers are an integral part of the garden team and get involved at every level, from gardening to guided tours, and from educational activities to administrative support.

Below left and right: The garden has a large and active band of volunteers who fulfil a multitude of essential functions: leading tours; gardening; meeting and greeting visitors and giving information; and helping with a wide range of education events, administrative tasks and special celebrations.